MEET The PETS

Presidential Animals from A to Z

By Cathy Collison & Janis Campbell

Illustrations by Wendy Popko

To my favorite pet-loving people, Steve, Colin, Andrew & Claire – J.C.

To Bill, Maggie & Robert, fellow travelers to presidential and pet places. – C.C.

To Ashley and Conner, may you continue to have compassion and respect for the creatures that share this planet with us. – W.P.

Text Copyright © 2021
By Cathy Collison and Janis Campbell

Illustrations Copyright © 2021
By Wendy Popko

ISBN 978-0-578-93733-5

Published by Campbell Collison Publishing

All rights reserved. First edition 2021.

Published and printed in the United States.

Book design by Marty Westman

Copy editing by Marcia Abramson

ON THE COVER

The cat and dog reporter on the cover of this book are gazing at a big circle with an eagle in the middle. This is our fun nod to the Presidential Seal, a symbol with a rich history.

When the president has some news to announce, you often see the commander in chief standing at a podium. And that podium – where you can speak through a microphone – usually has an image of the Presidential Seal. The historic symbol has been used on everything from Air Force One to the rug in the Oval Office.

Not all presidents have used the same image, but the bald eagle has always been present. President Franklin Roosevelt asked for the seal to be redesigned, including having the eagle head turn toward the olive branch in its talon, a sign of peace, and having 48 stars in the image for 48 states. It was President Harry Truman who made those changes official and gave the presidential order that a single design should be used for the seal. The seal was updated by President Dwight Eisenhower in 1959 and 1960 with two more stars to represent the new states of Alaska and Hawaii.

Eagles were even presidential pets! President James Buchanan was believed to have had two bald eagles as pets. Feathered friends often have been First Pets. President Thomas Jefferson liked mockingbirds and First Lady Dolley Madison had a parrot.

Animals don't run for election
But a history of First Pets shows quite a selection!
Short or tall, big or small,
These critters had the press tailing them all.

As reporters, we sure had fun sniffing out stories and digging up facts on presidential pets. Many pets made news, while others stayed out of the spotlight. Not every animal lived in the White House, but plenty became celebrities. We share some of the most interesting and popular stories from the pet beat. Read on from A to Z!

A

President Herbert Hoover's son Allan loved animals, especially their family dogs. He also had unusual pets – alligators, yikes! Those gators moved from the Hoovers' family home in Washington, D.C., to a new home at the National Zoo.

A is for alligator, a wild and wonderful reptile,
President Hoover's son had a pair for a while.
Before the family moved to Pennsylvania Avenue
It was "see you later, alligators," off to the zoo!

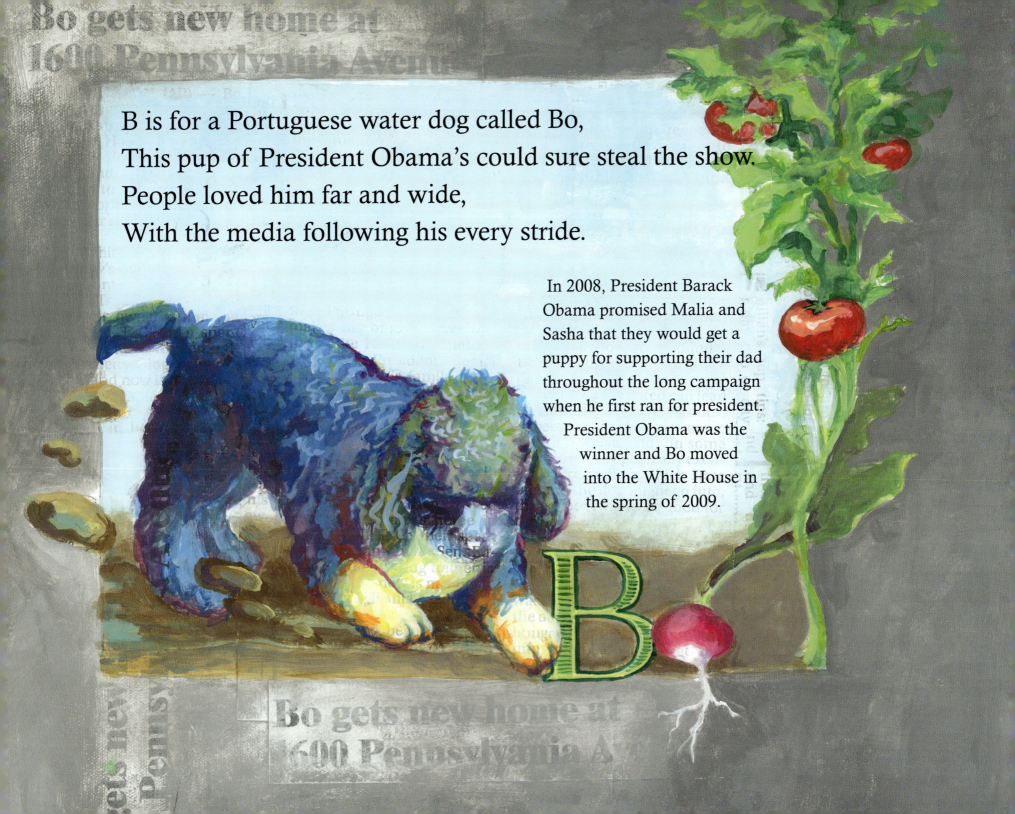

B is for a Portuguese water dog called Bo,
This pup of President Obama's could sure steal the show.
People loved him far and wide,
With the media following his every stride.

In 2008, President Barack Obama promised Malia and Sasha that they would get a puppy for supporting their dad throughout the long campaign when he first ran for president. President Obama was the winner and Bo moved into the White House in the spring of 2009.

C is for chickens, there was quite a flock.
At times, their eggs kept the White House in stock.
One thing we'd like to know:
How often did President Teddy Roosevelt's rooster crow?

A one-legged rooster was one of the many photographed pets of President Theodore "Teddy" Roosevelt and his family. You could call him the Animal Lover in Chief because over the years he welcomed more than 40 pets into his family.

D is for duiker, what on earth is that?
A little antelope from South Africa, which got the welcome mat.
President Coolidge was happy to give it a home,
Yet the antelope needed more space to roam.

The duiker was a gift to First Lady Grace Coolidge from a businessman who traveled overseas. The First Family was grateful but thought the White House did not have room for another pet. The animal was given a permanent home at the National Zoo. Only President Teddy Roosevelt and his family had more pets than the Coolidges.

E is for elephant, a gift to several presidents
Not well-suited for a White House residence.
One to President Reagan, which he greeted with elation,
A token of friendship from the Sri Lankan nation.

The memorial for Franklin Delano Roosevelt, who was called FDR, is the only presidential memorial on the National Mall that includes a pet. FDR had many canine companions but Fala, his Scottish terrier, was truly his favorite First Pet.

F is for Fala, President Franklin Roosevelt's cool canine,
A terrier friend so famous and fine.
In a bronze statue, you can see him today.
This faithful First Dog is here to stay.

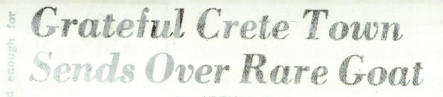

Grateful Crete Town Sends Over Rare Goat

By ARTHUR EDSON

G is for goat, a glorious one from Greece.
The gift to President Truman came with gratitude and peace.
A rare mountain climber from the Island of Crete,
Children visiting the zoo thought he was neat to meet.

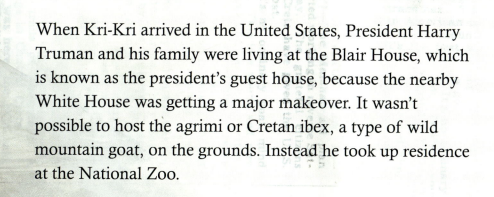

When Kri-Kri arrived in the United States, President Harry Truman and his family were living at the Blair House, which is known as the president's guest house, because the nearby White House was getting a major makeover. It wasn't possible to host the agrimi or Cretan ibex, a type of wild mountain goat, on the grounds. Instead he took up residence at the National Zoo.

H is for horse, there were more than a few.
President Washington's Nelson and Blueskin were two,
When done with their work, they retired to his farm
Where they were cherished and loved, and came to no harm.

The president used these two horses during the Revolutionary War, but Nelson was his most dependable horse in battles. Blueskin is the horse you see in famous paintings of President George Washington.

I is for Ike, called Old Ike by the press.
The grumpy ram could cause such distress!
President Wilson allowed him to wander the lawn,
Corralling the sheep and grazing at dawn.

Ike kept the lawn neat and tidy, along with the flock of White House sheep, grazing daily on the White House grass. The wool sheared from President Woodrow Wilson's sheep was auctioned off, earning thousands of dollars for the American Red Cross.

J is for Josiah, or Josh, for short.
This baby badger knew how to hold court.
Another critter in President Teddy Roosevelt's crew,
Until he found a home at New York's Bronx Zoo.

A girl named Pearl in Kansas gave a baby badger to President Roosevelt when he was on a cross-country train tour. Pearl asked the president to name the badger after her brother Josiah. The president thanked Pearl for her gift with a locket.

K is for Komodo dragons, fierce and cool creatures.
These long lizards are famous for their fantastic features.
Indonesia gave President George H. W. Bush a pair,
With detailed instructions on feeding and care.

The Komodo dragon is the largest lizard species in the world. They can grow up to 10 feet long and live to be 50 or older. The rare pair was placed at the Cincinnati Zoo, which specializes in caring for and breeding of these amazing creatures.

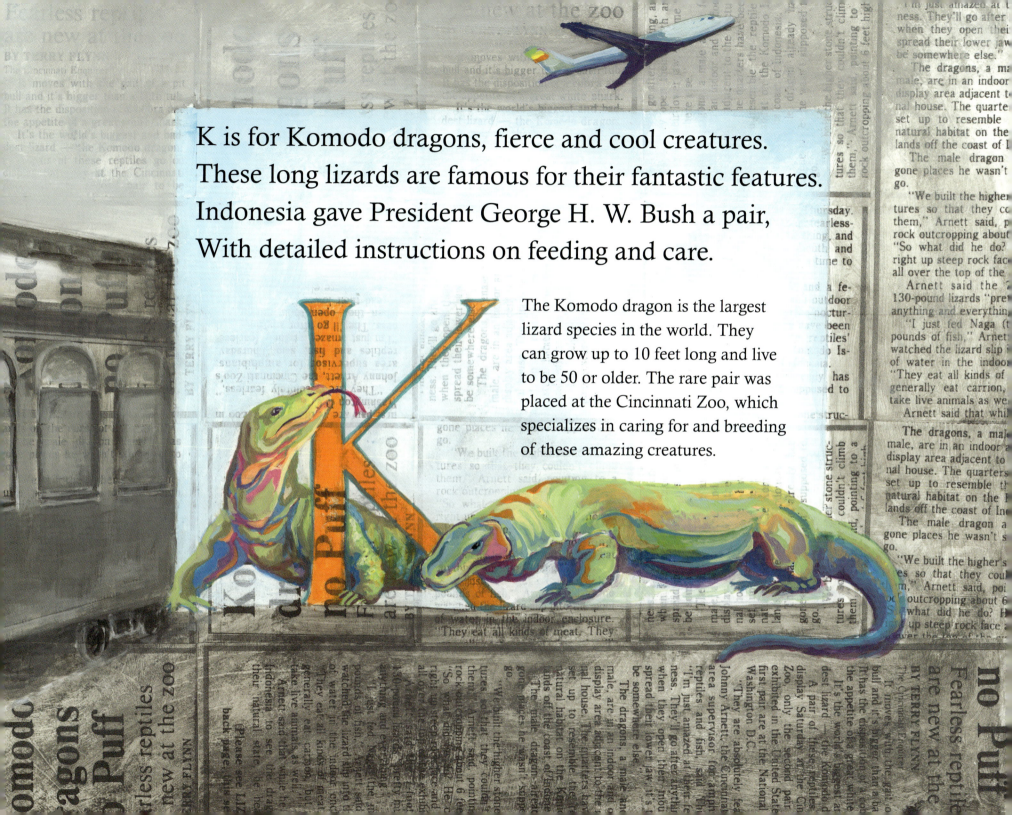

L is for Liberty, top dog for President Ford.
She romped and played, and was never bored.
Upstairs, downstairs, inside and out,
She was free to dash about.

First Lady Betty Ford shared a story in her book that President Ford once got locked out of the White House when he took the golden retriever out for a middle-of-the-night potty break. Liberty was expecting her first litter of puppies at the time.

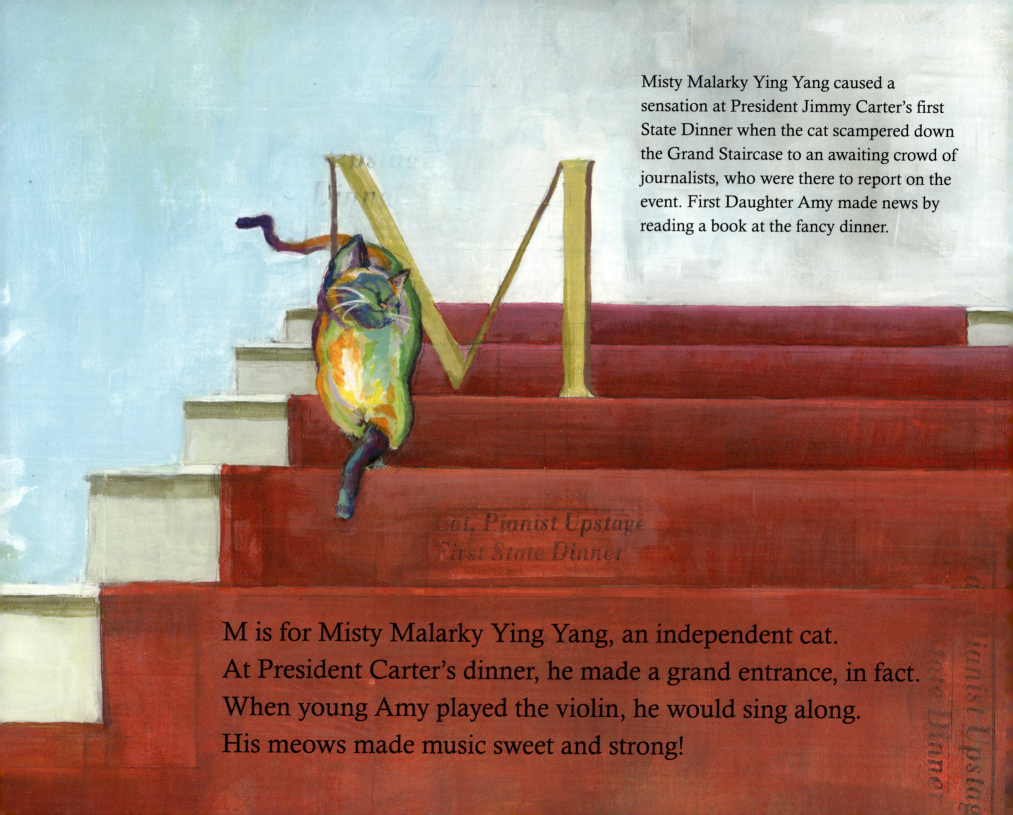

Misty Malarky Ying Yang caused a sensation at President Jimmy Carter's first State Dinner when the cat scampered down the Grand Staircase to an awaiting crowd of journalists, who were there to report on the event. First Daughter Amy made news by reading a book at the fancy dinner.

M is for Misty Malarky Ying Yang, an independent cat.
At President Carter's dinner, he made a grand entrance, in fact.
When young Amy played the violin, he would sing along.
His meows made music sweet and strong!

N is for the National Zoo, which has been a perfect place
For White House animals that need more space.
Thanks to President Cleveland, who gave it his OK,
The zoo welcomes animal ambassadors to this very day.

President Grover Cleveland signed a bill to officially start the zoo in 1889. Over the years, a few other zoos have received presidential pets, but most went to the Smithsonian's National Zoo, not far from the White House.

O is for opossum,
A critter most would not call awesome.
President Hoover adopted one, Billy was his name,
He became a school sports hero, deserving of his fame.

President Herbert Hoover adopted Billy as a pet after the critter was found on the White House grounds. Soon after, a high school baseball team in Maryland thought Billy might have been their lost mascot. Students visited the White House and realized Billy wasn't their mascot, but the president loaned the school his opossum and they won their next championship.

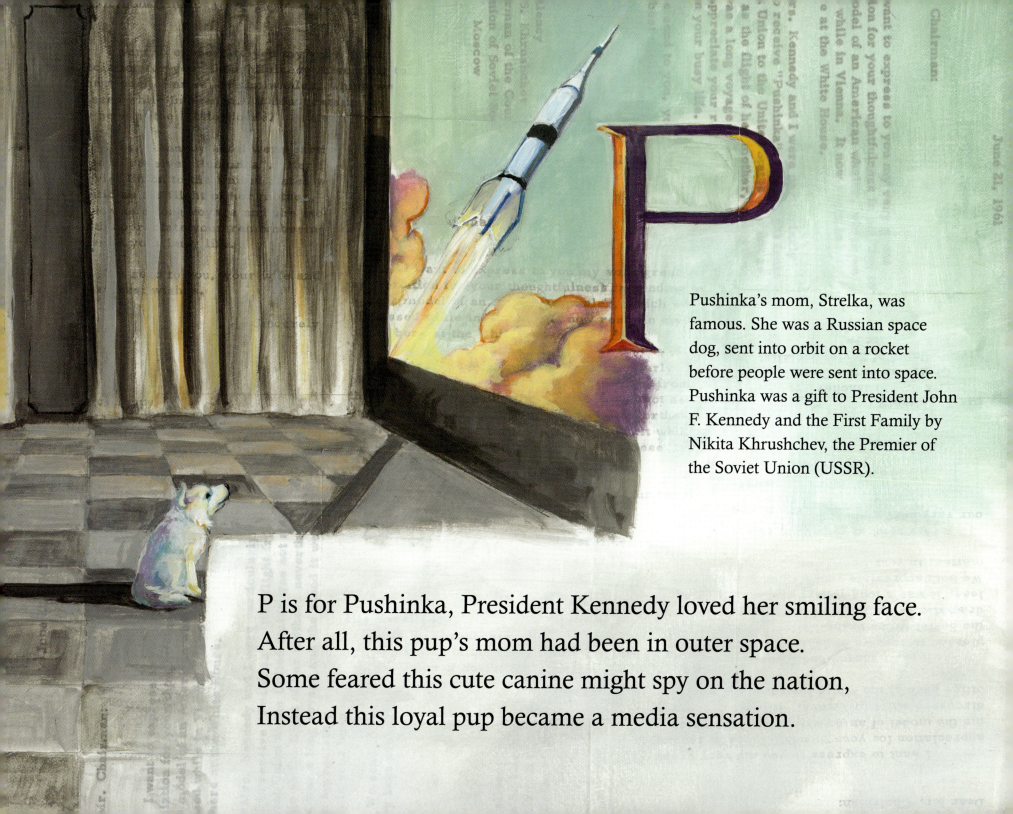

Pushinka's mom, Strelka, was famous. She was a Russian space dog, sent into orbit on a rocket before people were sent into space. Pushinka was a gift to President John F. Kennedy and the First Family by Nikita Khrushchev, the Premier of the Soviet Union (USSR).

P is for Pushinka, President Kennedy loved her smiling face.
After all, this pup's mom had been in outer space.
Some feared this cute canine might spy on the nation,
Instead this loyal pup became a media sensation.

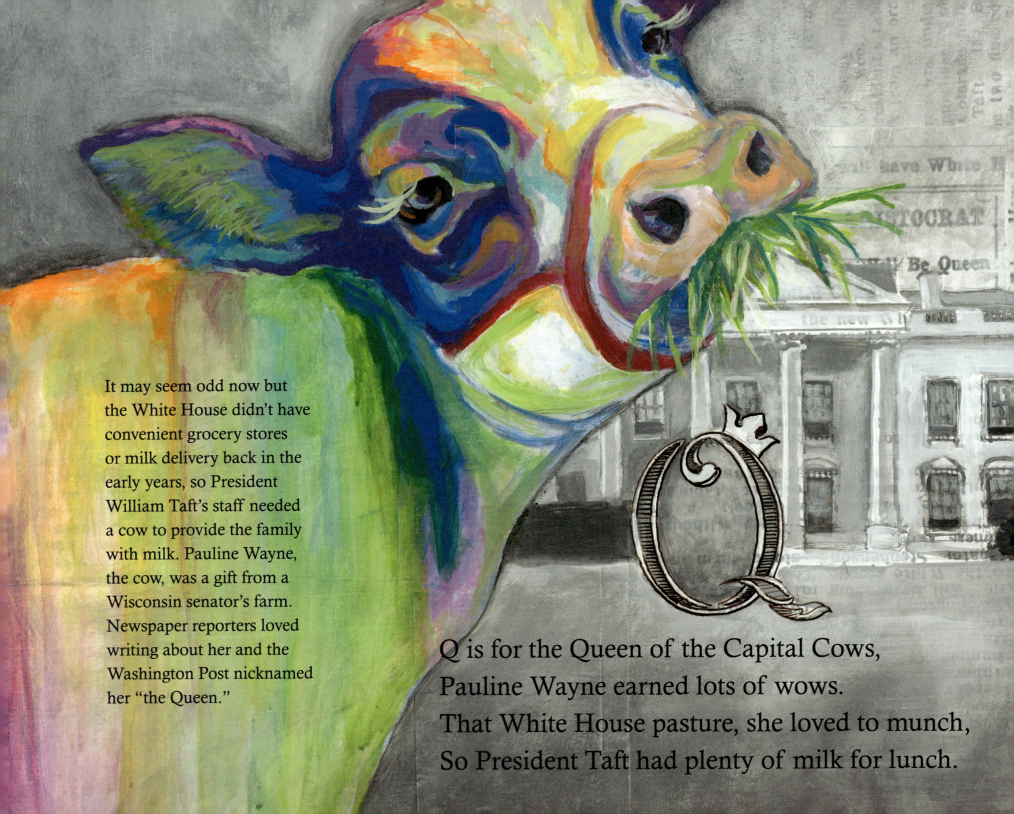

It may seem odd now but the White House didn't have convenient grocery stores or milk delivery back in the early years, so President William Taft's staff needed a cow to provide the family with milk. Pauline Wayne, the cow, was a gift from a Wisconsin senator's farm. Newspaper reporters loved writing about her and the Washington Post nicknamed her "the Queen."

Q is for the Queen of the Capital Cows,
Pauline Wayne earned lots of wows.
That White House pasture, she loved to munch,
So President Taft had plenty of milk for lunch.

R is for a raccoon, given to President Coolidge for dinner.
Named Rebecca, this charming critter ended up a winner.
First Lady Grace often took her out for a stroll,
And even let Rebecca join in the Easter Egg Roll.

A supporter from Mississippi gave a raccoon to President Calvin Coolidge for his Thanksgiving dinner, but the president had other ideas. First Lady Grace Coolidge was an animal lover and was charmed by the raccoon. She adopted Rebecca as a treasured pet and took her to public events like the Easter Egg Roll, which is held every year on the White House lawn. Rebecca even accompanied the family on vacations, including to their summer home in the Black Hills of South Dakota.

S is for Socks, President Clinton's cool cat.
As a website guide for children, he was all that.
Even today, the story of Socks
Is presidential history that truly rocks!

Socks was the First Cat that introduced children to a special White House website just for kids. Socks was one popular cat. He received a special tribute from the White House chef in the traditional holiday gingerbread house, which was called "House of Socks." First Lady Hillary Clinton reported that Socks couldn't resist and tried to take a nibble!

T is for turkey, delivered for President Lincoln's meal.
His son Tad wanted no part of that deal!
So the president took the bird off the table,
And there began a political fable.

Many people date the tradition of a president pardoning a turkey at Thanksgiving to President Abraham Lincoln, but this turkey was offered as a Christmas meal. His son Tad named the turkey Jack and convinced his father to keep the bird as a pet. The president, also an animal lover, agreed.

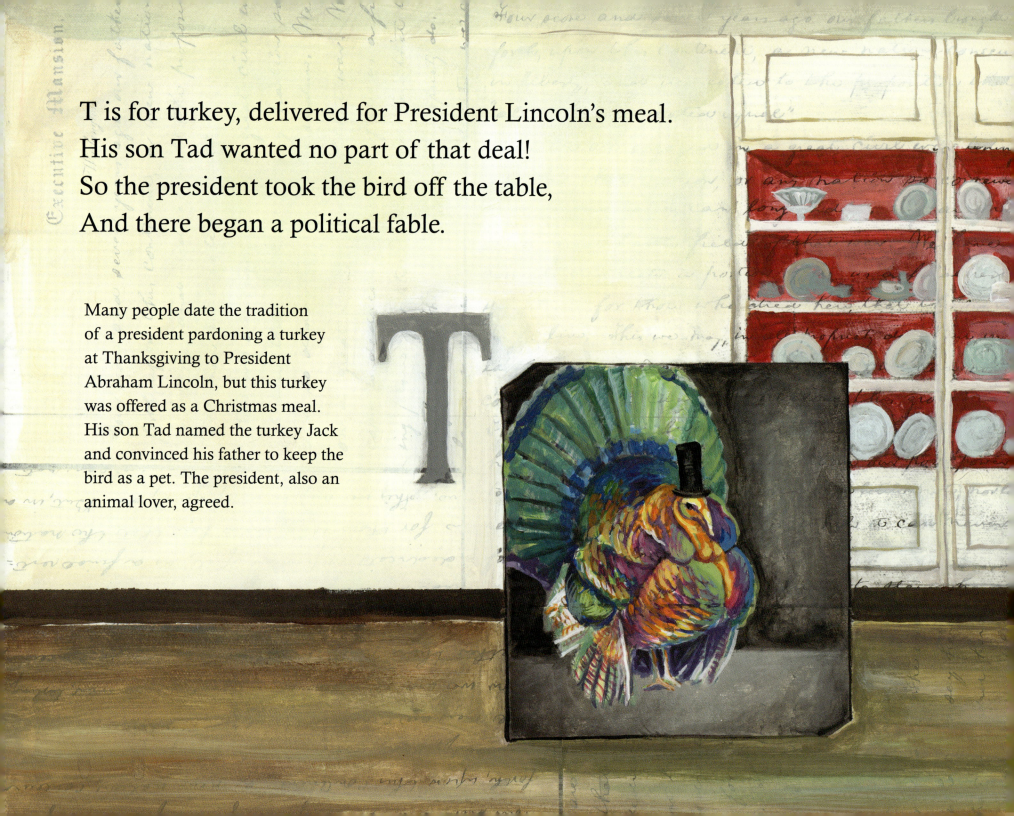

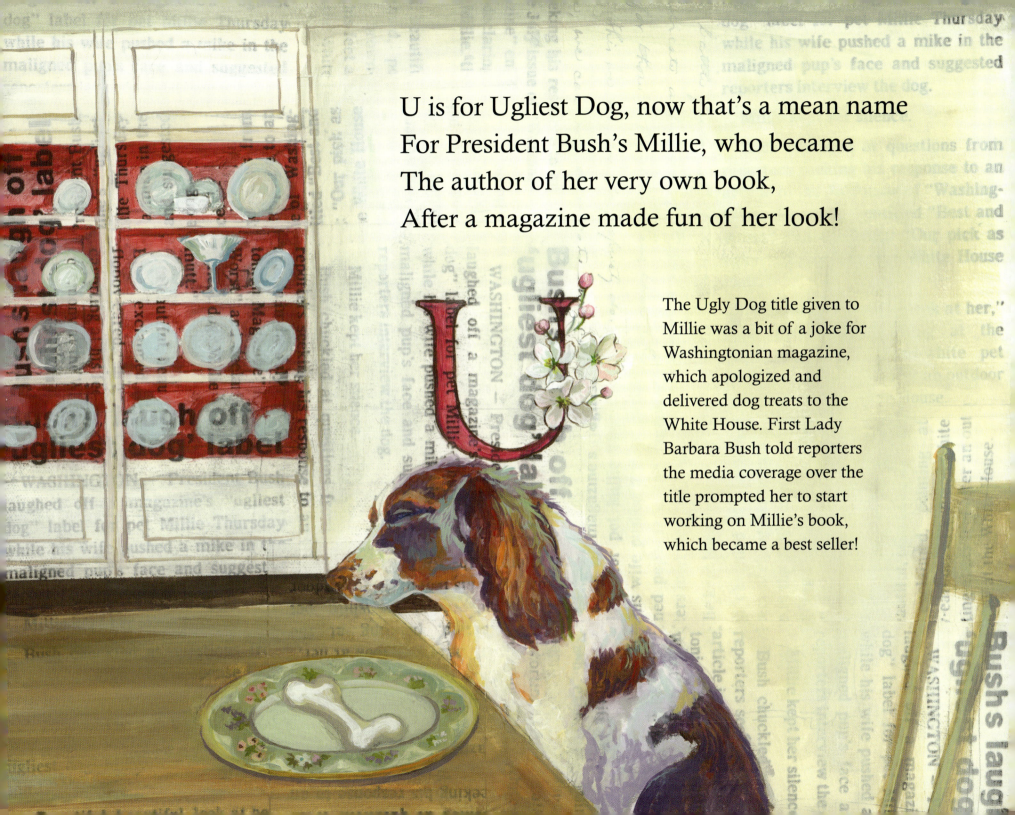

U is for Ugliest Dog, now that's a mean name
For President Bush's Millie, who became
The author of her very own book,
After a magazine made fun of her look!

The Ugly Dog title given to Millie was a bit of a joke for Washingtonian magazine, which apologized and delivered dog treats to the White House. First Lady Barbara Bush told reporters the media coverage over the title prompted her to start working on Millie's book, which became a best seller!

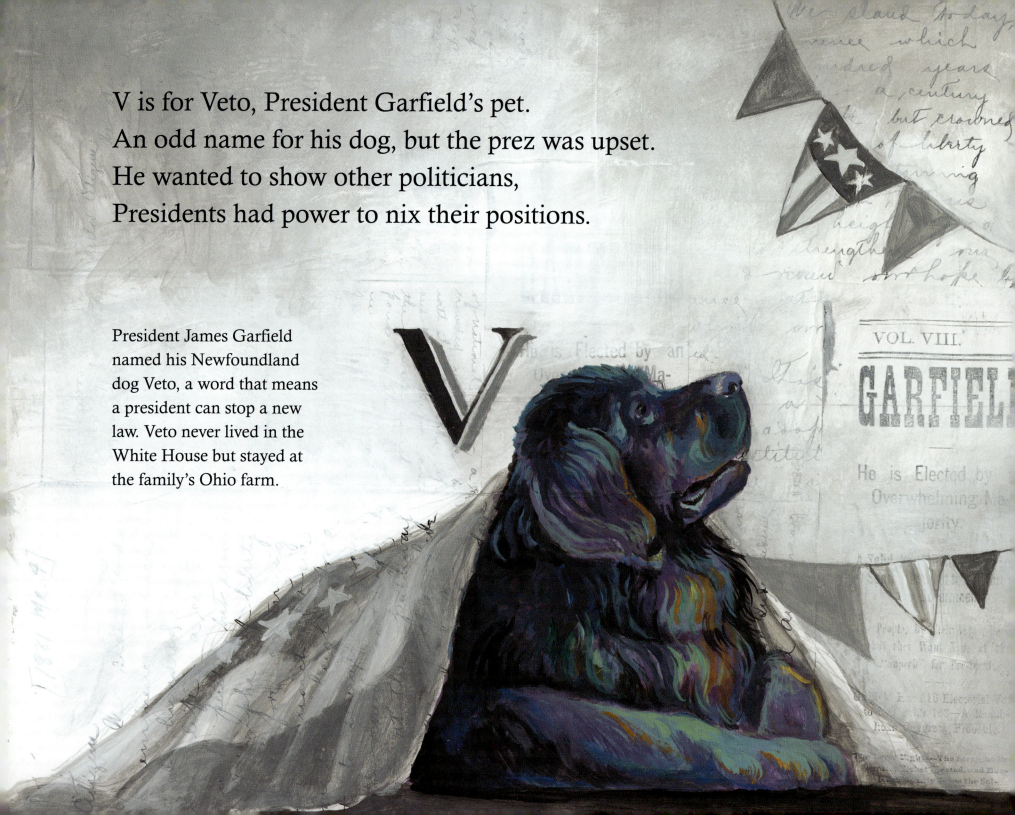

V is for Veto, President Garfield's pet.
An odd name for his dog, but the prez was upset.
He wanted to show other politicians,
Presidents had power to nix their positions.

President James Garfield named his Newfoundland dog Veto, a word that means a president can stop a new law. Veto never lived in the White House but stayed at the family's Ohio farm.

Wallabies can hop over 5 feet, so maybe President Coolidge knew the critter given to him would do better at the National Zoo. Because the Coolidges were known to love animals, they received many critters as gifts.

W is for wallaby, a cousin of the kangaroo.
The present to President Coolidge caused a big to-do.
He had so many exotic pets that this critter, too,
Was happily sent to the National Zoo!

X is for X-ray, a check for a bone break,
Something President Biden's foot had to take.
A slip playing with his dog, but he was OK
And with mighty Major he will continue to play.

President Joe Biden had a minor injury to his foot while playing with Major, his frisky German shepherd pup, before taking office. Major was first fostered and then adopted by the Bidens from an animal shelter in Delaware. Major is the first presidential pet adopted from an animal shelter.

Y

Y is for Yuki, a true rescue mix.
Left at a gas station, he was in a fix.
Later President Johnson, known as LBJ,
Adopted the dog and made his day!

Yuki could be considered the first rescue dog in the White House. President Lyndon B. Johnson's daughter Luci found him on Thanksgiving Day at a gas station in Texas. Luci took the little dog home but later gave him to her dad as a birthday gift. LBJ loved Yuki and the canine became his constant companion.

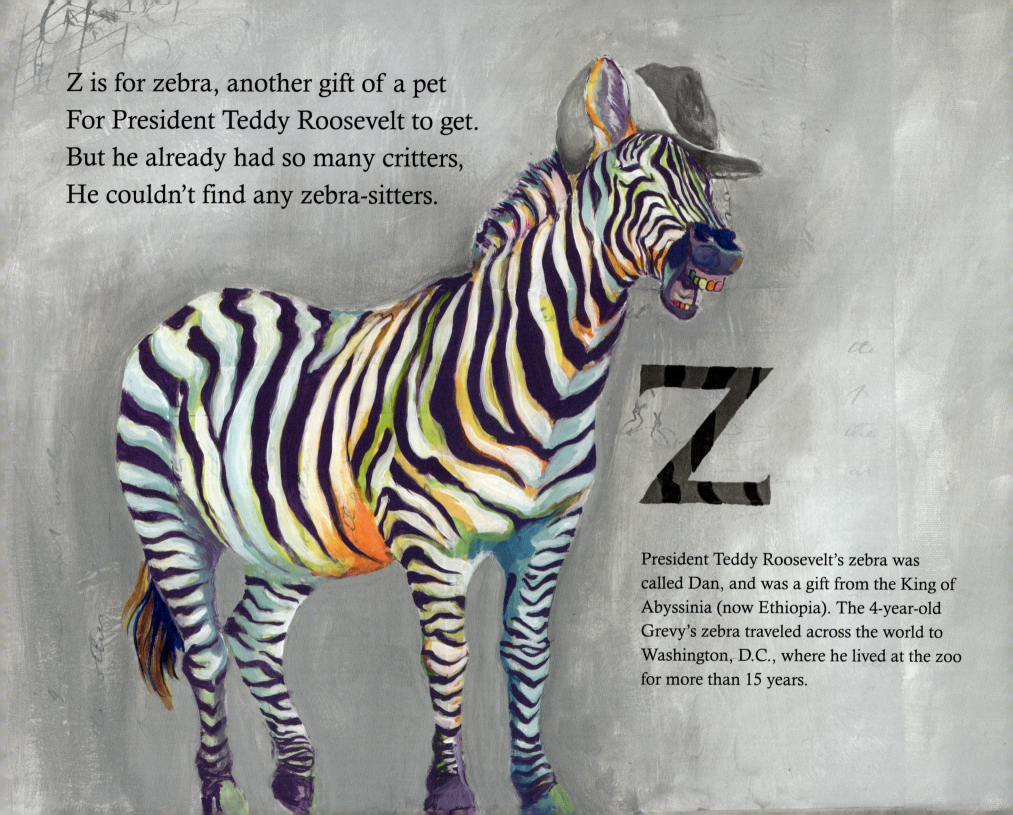

Z is for zebra, another gift of a pet
For President Teddy Roosevelt to get.
But he already had so many critters,
He couldn't find any zebra-sitters.

President Teddy Roosevelt's zebra was called Dan, and was a gift from the King of Abyssinia (now Ethiopia). The 4-year-old Grevy's zebra traveled across the world to Washington, D.C., where he lived at the zoo for more than 15 years.

United States Presidents

Only two presidents while in office did not have any pets that were recorded in history. They were President Chester Arthur and President Donald Trump. Here is the complete list of presidents.

1. George Washington
   1789-1797
2. John Adams
   1797-1801
3. Thomas Jefferson
   1801-1809
4. James Madison
   1809-1817
5. James Monroe
   1817-1825
6. John Quincy Adams
   1825-1829
7. Andrew Jackson
   1829-1837
8. Martin Van Buren
   1837-1841
9. William Henry Harrison
   1841
10. John Tyler
    1841-1845
11. James K. Polk
    1845-1849
12. Zachary Taylor
    1849-1850
13. Millard Filmore
    1850-1853
14. Franklin Pierce
    1853-1857
15. James Buchanan
    1857-1861
16. Abraham Lincoln
    1861-1865
17. Andrew Johnson
    1865-1869
18. Ulysses S. Grant
    1869-1877
19. Rutherford B. Hayes
    1877-1881
20. James Garfield
    1881
21. Chester Arthur
    1881-1885
22. Grover Cleveland
    1885-1889
23. Benjamin Harrison
    1889-1893
24. Grover Cleveland
    1893-1897
25. William McKinley
    1897-1901
26. Theodore Roosevelt
    1901-1909
27. William Taft
    1909-1913
28. Woodrow Wilson
    1913-1921
29. Warren G. Harding
    1921-1923
30. Calvin Coolidge
    1923-1929
31. Herbert Hoover
    1929-1933
32. Franklin D. Roosevelt
    1933-1945
33. Harry S. Truman
    1945-1953
34. Dwight Eisenhower
    1953-1961
35. John F. Kennedy
    1961-1963
36. Lyndon B. Johnson
    1963-1969
37. Richard Nixon
    1969-1974
38. Gerald R. Ford
    1974-1977
39. Jimmy Carter
    1977-1981
40. Ronald Reagan
    1981-1989
41. George H.W. Bush
    1989-1993
42. Bill Clinton
    1993-2001
43. George W. Bush
    2001-2009
44. Barack Obama
    2009-2017
45. Donald Trump
    2017-2021
46. Joseph Biden
    2021-

Photo Courtesy of George W. Bush Presidential Center

On April 25, 2013, five presidents attended the dedication of the George W. Bush Presidential Library and Museum. From left, President Barack Obama, President George W. Bush, President Bill Clinton, President George H.W. Bush and President Jimmy Carter.

**What is black and white and red all over?
A blushing zebra?
No, a newspaper.**

Get to Know the White House

Throughout the book, you will see locations in and around the White House. Here is a guide to the presidential places shown in the book.

The Kitchen Garden was started on the South Lawn by First Lady Michelle Obama in the spring of 2009 to encourage healthy eating. It was the first vegetable garden since First Lady Eleanor Roosevelt's Victory Garden during World War II.

The view of the White House from the South Lawn became even more familiar to the public during President Calvin Coolidge's term because that is when media coverage of the White House really took off. The duiker, a gift to the First Lady, became a celebrity at the National Zoo, but never galloped into fame on the South Lawn.

Over the years, First Families have made their mark, with handprints and names imprinted on stepping stones to decorate the Children's Garden, which was started by President Lyndon B. Johnson and his wife, Lady Bird. Their grandchildren Patrick and Lucinda were the first to leave their prints (handprints for Lucinda, footprints for Patrick). The tradition was followed by most presidential grandchildren, including President Jimmy Carter's. Of course, the small garden could never have room for a pachyderm print.

The statue of President Franklin Delano Roosevelt with his dog, Fala, is one of many memorials on the nearby National Mall, which is often called "America's Front Yard."

President Harry S. Truman opened the first bowling alley in the White House in the spring of 1947. Even though he did not bowl much, his staff used the two-lane alley.

Ike and the other sheep grazed on the South Lawn. Many call this the backyard of the White House. It's a popular place for White House events.

President Ulysses S. Grant installed the current South Lawn Fountain, which to this day is a beautiful attraction on the White House grounds. First Dogs have been known to take a dip, including Liberty.

Misty Malarky Ying Yang once made a grand entrance on the Grand Staircase, getting the press's attention. The red-carpeted Grand Staircase is mainly used for ceremonies for foreign guests attending a State Dinner.

The National Zoo opened in 1891. Famous landscape architect Frederick Law Olmsted designed it within Rock Creek Park, about three miles from the White House. The full name today is the Smithsonian's National Zoo and Conservation Biology Institute.

The 42-seat movie theater was built in 1942 in the East Wing. It's where the First Family and special guests can enjoy movies.

The Queen of Capital Cows, Pauline Wayne, ruled when she grazed on the White House grounds. Shown here, the North Lawn. The North Entrance to the White House is the formal entrance, and the steps may have a red carpet put down when a foreign leader or special guest arrives.

Rebecca the raccoon was a special host at one Easter Egg Roll, an event that is held yearly on the South Lawn of the White House. The South Lawn is part of President's Park, an area of 85 acres that includes the White House grounds.

During President Bill Clinton's first term, the House of Socks was the name of the gingerbread house created for the annual holiday decorations. The house was displayed on a fancy historic table in the State Dining Room. The tradition of a themed gingerbread house began when President Richard Nixon was in office.

The China Room is where the State Dinner china is displayed. Engraved at the top of the cabinet is "China Used by the Presidents." Usually, this room would be off limits to pets, but in July 1991, First Lady Barbara Bush helped Millie make a pawprint for a greeting card there.

True, the zebra given to President Teddy Roosevelt, didn't live in the White House, but he was one of the many Roosevelt animals to make news. Teddy Roosevelt was the first president to add a press room in the renovation of offices that would later become the West Wing.

Extra! Extra! Read All About Them!

These alpha-pet pages from A to Z are just a starting point for learning about presidential pets. Our notebooks are full of fun and surprising facts.

A tale with bite

In gator news, President John Quincy Adams was rumored to have alligators given to him by a French general, the Marquis de Lafayette – or maybe they were just house guests accompanying the visiting war hero of the American Revolution. Either way, the story seems to be more legend than fact. However, the general did travel the country, visiting every state from 1824 to 1825, and it is believed that he probably did encounter alligators during his trip to America.

Turkey talk

Food was a popular gift to give the early presidents. The gift could even be a live animal that the White House kitchen would cook and serve to the First Family for dinner. President Abraham Lincoln was given a turkey for the family's Christmas meal. As you read earlier, that turkey became a pet. This act of turkey kindness is often considered the beginning of the American tradition of turkey pardoning. President Lincoln did proclaim Thanksgiving as an official holiday, but nothing in the proclamation was about sparing turkeys.

After that, other presidents often had newspapers and even television following a turkey sparing each November. But it was President George H. W. Bush who first spoke the words making the presidential pardoning of the national Thanksgiving turkey even more official. Now every year, the president spares a turkey or two! It has become a well-publicized event with citizens sometimes voting on which turkey will get the official pardon. Either way, the pardoned turkeys get to live out their days in peace in a variety of places. Pardoned turkeys in the past have even gone to Disney World, as well as other farms and parks.

A dashing dog

Another First Dog to know about is Laddie Boy, the pet of President Warren G. Harding. Laddie Boy became world famous, appearing in many newspapers and magazine stories. To this very day, he is often called the first celebrity pet. President Harding loved his Laddie Boy so much that he had 1,000 small statues made in Laddie Boy's likeness to give away to supporters and fans. Laddie Boy still made the newspaper headlines even after the president died in 1923. The dog went to live in Massachusetts with Henry Barker, who was a favorite of Laddie Boy's and a former Secret Service guard of the president.

There was also a life-size statue made of Laddie Boy. It was special because it was created in part from more than 19,000 pennies collected by newsboys, who were boys who sold or delivered newspapers. It was a fitting tribute because President Harding was a newspaper man. He began his career as an apprentice in his teens and later bought and ran an Ohio newspaper.

Horsing around in the White House

Many early presidents had horses, and of course, before automobiles, the First Families used a horse and carriage for transportation. Throughout the decades, several families also had horses as pets. President Teddy Roosevelt was an accomplished rider and Algonquin, a pet for his children, made headlines. In the spring of 1903, newspapers shared the story that when Archie was starting to recover from the measles, White House staff member Charles Reeder took Algonquin up the elevator to the second floor so he could have a bedroom visit. Later stories often said Archie's brothers Quentin and Kermit came up with the idea, but that was not likely. The Boston Globe also reported on Algonquin starring in the "Roosevelt Circus" in 1906 when Archie performed for the family bareback on the pony, riding around a ring, with Quentin and Ethel, their sister, also performing in other stunts.

In the 1960s, accomplished rider and First Lady Jacqueline Kennedy shared her love of riding with First Daughter Caroline. Young Caroline was often photographed on the White House grounds on her favorite pony, Macaroni. Caroline was also given another pony, Tex, by Vice President Lyndon B. Johnson. A third pony, Leprechaun, was given to the Kennedys by the president of Ireland.

Puppy love

President Barack Obama made his 2008 election victory speech in Grant Park in Chicago, saying to his daughters: "I love you both more than you can imagine. You have earned the puppy that is coming with us." Bo joined the First Family at the White House in the spring of 2009. Sunny, their second Portuguese Water Dog, was added to the family in the summer of 2013. Why Portuguese Water Dogs?

They are considered hypoallergenic, which means they are pets well-suited to people with allergies, including First Daughter Malia.

Fake news!

President Franklin Delano Roosevelt, who was nicknamed FDR, took his beloved Scottish terrier Fala on his travels by car, train and ship. Fala even had a specially designed Navy coat, which is on display at FDR's Hyde Park home in New York. Fala made big news when a political rival made up a story that the first pooch had been left behind on a presidential trip, resulting in a very costly rescue. That never happened! FDR made a speech that scolded people for spreading fake news and worse, attacking his beloved pet.

A dog's-eye view

You could call Barney the first video reporter in the White House. Barney and his sidekick Miss Beazley belonged to President George W. Bush and his family. They were Scottish terriers who made plenty of news, with Barney once even nipping a reporter. Barney also got behind the camera with the now famous "Barney Cam" videos, giving a dog's-eye view of the White House. The series of Barney Cam videos made the terrier an internet sensation. People still watch the videos today.

President Biden brings pets back to the White House

New presidents always make news but when President Joe Biden was elected, the media went wild over the return of pets to the White House after four years of no furry friends. Major Biden made headlines as the first shelter dog living in the White House.

What was Major's story? Cory Topel of the Delaware Humane Association shared that Major was one of six young puppies that were brought to the humane association after being exposed to something toxic in the owners' home. The puppies were given up to the humane association for care and medical treatment that saved the lives of Major and his siblings. A Facebook post for funding help caught the eye of Ashley Biden, who is now the First Daughter and who shared it with her parents.

Cory says, "Joe Biden came to DHA, unannounced with two of his grandkids, to see the puppies just like any other normal person would. Joe and Jill Biden first fostered Major until they eventually adopted him…and the rest is history." Cory and the team at the humane association, as well as pet rescues and shelters across the country, are excited that Major's story has been big news. Cory says, "We hope Major's story will help shine a light on the importance of adopting from shelters."

Reporters were doggedly following the story of pets returning to the White House. Major's antics overshadowed Champ, the older German shepherd that had been part of their family since Joe Biden served as vice president.

The media was covering everything from the in-dogeration, a celebration for Major that raised funds for the Delaware Humane Association, to a couple of minor biting incidents. There was even a big scoop on poop, when one of the dogs went poo in the hallway on a day when reporters were waiting to talk to First Lady Jill Biden. The press also kept busy sniffing around the news of a cat for the Bidens. At press time for this book, the First Feline was said to be waiting in the wings.

Sadly, the press also covered the announcement from the White House in June 2021 that beloved First Dog Champ had died. The White House statement from President Joe Biden and First Lady Jill Biden said that "….he was our constant, cherished companion during the last 13 years and was adored by the entire Biden family. Even as Champ's strength waned in the last month, when we came into a room, he would immediately pull himself up, his tail always wagging, and nuzzle us for an ear scratch or a belly rub. Wherever we were, he wanted to be, and everything was instantly better when he was next to us. He loved nothing more than curling up at our feet in front of a fire at the end of the day, joining us as a comforting presence in meetings, or sunning himself in the White House garden…"

GLOSSARY

These definitions reflect the way words were used in this book.

Ambassador: Official U.S. ambassadors represent the nation in other countries. The word also means any person (or pet!) that represents a group, person or activity.

Beat: An assigned area or topic to cover. A reporter doing stories only about the White House would be on the White House beat.

Bill: A draft of a proposed law presented to lawmakers, such as the U.S. Congress.

Campaign: In politics, it's the series of events, advertisements and publicity made in the effort to be elected.

Cherish: To love, protect and care for someone or something.

First Dog, First Cat: We used these words playfully to describe the pets belonging to the president or his family. The wife of the president has the title of First Lady. Recently you will also see the more informal terms like First Family or First Pets.

Foster: To care for a rescue or shelter pet temporarily before it is placed with a permanent home.

Headline: A headline is the title of a news story. If you look carefully at the illustrations, some headlines show through in the collage.

Media: This is the term used to describe all forms of communication, including newspapers and magazines, television and radio, and the internet or social media such as Twitter and Instagram.

Nix: To deny permission or just say no to something. Newspaper headlines used to use this term in the past because it was a very short word.

Pardon: An official pardon from the president means that someone charged with or convicted of a crime is now free. In our book, we talk about the tradition of the turkey pardon.

Press: The people who report on news, whether working for newspapers, magazines, television, or social media.

Reporter: A reporter interviews a person to get information that readers or viewers do not know. Then they put together a news report. On the first page of this book, you will see a cat and dog reporter.

Scoop: To get a story first before other competing reporters do.

State dinner: A formal dinner held by the president at the White House for foreign leaders and special guests.

Veto: To say no or reject a proposed bill.

About the artist:

Wendy Popko, an award-winning visual artist, is an accomplished outdoor muralist, a painter of pet portraits and a picture book illustrator. Wendy has displayed her artwork at museums, libraries and twice in ArtPrize in Grand Rapids, Michigan, including the artwork for this book. She has participated in the Detroit Institute of Arts Partners in Public Art (PIPA) program. Wendy is a longtime metro Detroit resident, and lives with her husband and two children, and their rescue dog Bailey. Wendy is co-chair of her local arts commission and a trustee on her library board.

About the authors:

Cathy Collison and Janis Campbell have been friends and writing partners for more than 25 years. They worked at the Detroit Free Press together for many years and have contributed to more than a dozen book projects. Both Janis and Cathy are history tourists and animal lovers.

Cathy lives with her husband in metro Detroit. Cathy, a feline fan, especially loves the big cats and the red pandas at the Detroit Zoo, where she volunteers as a docent.

Janis lives in northern Michigan with her husband and her shelter dog, Hamilton. For more than a decade she has coordinated a holiday pet food drive for the local animal shelter.

SOURCES AND SINCERE THANKS

As animal lovers, it was a joy to immerse ourselves in the history of presidential pets. Newspaper archives, historical documents and digitized collections from presidential libraries and many books guided our research. In addition to the people we thank on this page, we are listing additional sources we want to acknowledge. We found a wealth of information in the Library of Congress and many presidential libraries and home sites to explore without leaving our homes.

Books

Inside the White House: Stories from the World's Most Famous Residence by Noel Grove with William B. Bushong and Joel D. Treese with the White House Historical Association (National Geographic, 2015)

Pets at the White House: 50 Years of President and Their Pets by Jennifer B. Pickens (Fife & Drum Press, 2012)

Presidential Pets: The Weird, Wacky, Little, Big, Scary, Strange Animals That Have Lived in the White House by Julia Moberg (Charlesbridge Publishing, 2012)

The White House: Its Historic Furnishings and First Families by Betty C. Monkman (Abbeville Press, 2000)

Wackiest White House Pets by Gibbs Davis (Scholastic Press, 2004)

Collage Contributions

Primary sources are a great resource for history. Newspapers in particular are a wonderful window to the past. Many libraries, including the Library of Congress, make digitized newspapers available online. So do content services such as newspapers.com, which we found an invaluable source in our research into how presidential pets made headlines. In fact, presidential pets continue to be big news. On each illustrated page, our artist has incorporated documents, letters and newspaper articles within her illustrations. Here are the credits for the documents and newspapers used with permission and sincere thanks.

Newspaper and document credits

Page 4: Letter to Lou Henry Hoover from Philippi Harding, May 18, 1921.

Page 5: "Bo gets new home at 1600 Pennsylvania Avenue," (Headline), Carroll Daily Times Herald, April 14, 2009.

Page 6: Letter to Kermit from President Teddy Roosevelt, May 10, 1903.

Page 7: "Two Cub Lions Are Intended for Coolidge," © Detroit Free Press-USA TODAY NETWORK, April 27, 1927.

Pages 8-9: "Amy Carter to get baby elephant," © Muncie Evening Press-USA TODAY NETWORK, April 1, 1977.

Page 10: Typewritten copy of the speech President Franklin Delano Roosevelt would give September 23, 1944 to the Teamsters Union.

Page 11: "Grateful Crete Town Sends Over Rare Goats," © Arizona Republic-USA TODAY NETWORK, July 16, 1950.

Page 12: President George Washington, George Washington Farewell Address, September 17, 1796, Library of Congress Manuscript Division: George Washington Papers.

Page 13: "Ike, President Wilson's Famous Tobacco-Chewing Ram, Dies of the Infirmities of Old Age," (Headline), Waco News-Tribune, August 14, 1927.

Page 14: "The President's Visit, Had a Fine Time in Western Springs," The Western Times, Sharon Springs, Kansas, May 8, 1903.

Page 15: "Komodo dragons no Puff," © The Cincinnati Enquirer-USA Network, July 13,1990.

Page 16: "Liberty's paw-tograph" letter by Susan Ford, 1976.

Page 17: "Cat, Pianist Upstage First State Dinner," (Headline) The Item, Sumter, South Carolina, February 15, 1977.

Page 18-19: House of Representatives Bill H.R. 11810, December 17, 1888.

Page 20: Letter to President Herbert Hoover from The Athletic Association, Robert M. Venemann, William E. Robinson, Hyattsville High School, July 12, 1929 and letter from President Herbert Hoover to Robert M. Venemann, Hyattsville High School, July 13, 1929.

Page 21: Letter to Nikita S. Khrushchev from President John F. Kennedy, June 21, 1961.

Page 22: "Pauline Is An Aristocrat, New White House Milker Will Be Queen of Capital Cows," Washington Post, May 29, 1910.

Page 23: "Meet Rebecca!" The Cincinnati Enquirer, December 25, 1926.

Page 24-25: "Socks Upstages Clintons," © Green Bay Press Gazette-USA TODAY NETWORK, December 21, 1996.

Page 26: President Abraham Lincoln's Gettysburg Address, Nicolay copy, 1863, Library of Congress, Abraham Lincoln Papers, Manuscript Division.

Page 27: "Bushes Laugh Off 'Ugliest Dog' Label," © Poughkeepsie Journal-USA TODAY NETWORK, June 30, 1989.

Page 28: "Garfield, He Is Elected By An Overwhelming Majority," Bismarck Tribune, November 5, 1880.

Page 29: "Coolidge Accepts Wallaby After Cautious Inquiry Offer of Gift of a Kind of Kangaroo Causes Hasty Trip to the Dictionary," St. Louis Post-Dispatch, September 22, 1925.

Page 30: "2 pooches to get paw-some new digs in the White House," © Detroit Free Press-USA TODAY NETWORK, November 11, 2020.

Page 31: Bess Abel letter to class, November 14, 1967; Indianapolis, Indiana classroom, grade 4 letters to Yuki, October 30, 1967.

Page 32: President Teddy Roosevelt letter to Quentin Roosevelt, June 12, 1904.

Page 33: Photo courtesy of the George W. Bush Presidential Center. Photo of 5 living presidents at the dedication of the George W. Bush Presidential Library and Museum.

Bibliography

Websites

www.newspapers.com

www.presidentialpetmuseum.com

www.whitehousehistory.org The White House Historical Association

www.loc.gov Library of Congress, also see Chronicling America within the Library of Congress website for the historic newspapers collection

www.archives.gov The National Archives and Records Administration

Presidential libraries, research centers

www.bushcenter.org George W. Bush Presidential Center

www.georgewbushlibrary.smu.edu George W. Bush Presidential Library and Museum

www.clintonlibrary.gov President William J. Clinton Presidential Library & Museum

www.forbeslibrary.org Calvin Coolidge Presidential Library and Museum at the Forbes Library

www.coolidgefoundation.org The Calvin Coolidge Presidential Foundation

www.fordlibrarymuseum.gov Gerald R. Ford Presidential Library & Museum

www.hoover.archives.gov Herbert Hoover Presidential Library and Museum

www.lbjlibrary.org Lyndon B. Johnson Presidential Library

www.jfklibrary.org John F. Kennedy Presidential Library and Museum

www.fdrlibrary.org Franklin D. Roosevelt Presidential Library and Museum

www.obama.org The Obama Foundation

www.trlibrary.com The Theodore Roosevelt Library Project

www.dickinsonstate.edu/about/theodore-roosevelt-center/ Theodore Roosevelt Center at Dickinson State University in North Dakota

Thanks to these people:

Jamie Atkins, RCP Artist Services Inc.
Bob Bayer, Atwater Brewery manager, and the team at Atwater Brewery in Grand Rapids, our ArtPrize venue host
Rodger Beyer and Lisa Ceplina, and the team at Worzalla
Steve Boggs, editor of Waco Tribune-Herald, Waco, Texas
Kirsten Strigel Carter, supervisory archivist, FDR Presidential Library and Museum
Pamela Casey, architecture archivist, Avery Architecture and Fine Arts Library, Columbia University
Kinsey Clemmer, associate, communications, George W. Bush Presidential Center
Drew Cuthbertson, manager of Customer Service at Imagn, part of the USA Today Network
Stacy Davis, archivist, Gerald R. Ford Presidential Library
Jenna De Graffenried, archivist, Lyndon B. Johnson Presidential Library
Michelle Desmond, archives tech, John F. Kennedy Presidential Library
Will Elsbury, reference librarian, Library of Congress
Michelle M. Frauenberger, museum collections manager/registrar, Franklin D. Roosevelt Presidential Library
Jessica Fredericks, director of communications, White House Historical Association
Melanie Gilbert, author and encourager
Erik Johnson, Theodore Roosevelt Presidential Center, Dickinson State University
Vince Johnson, publisher of the Sumter Item, Sumter, South Carolina
David Lace, publisher, the Western Times, Sharon Springs, Kansas
Jacqui Lipton, our literary agent and encourager
Matt Porter, communications officer, John F. Kennedy Library Foundation
Thomas Schwartz, director, Herbert J. Hoover Presidential Library
Cory Topel, marketing manager, Delaware Humane Association
Allison Trulock, associate archivist, Office of Art and Archives, Office of the Clerk, U.S. House of Representatives
Anne Wheeler, communications director, LBJ Presidential Library & Foundation
Ann Wilson, publisher, Carroll Daily Times Herald, Carroll, Iowa
Craig Wright, senior archivist, Herbert J. Hoover Presidential Library
Lewis Wyman, reference librarian, Library of Congress